The Seven E's of Reading fo

Also in this series

The Seven C's of Positive Behaviour Management
The Seven P's of Brilliant Voice Usage
The Seven R's of Great Group Work
The Seven T's of Practical Differentiation

Also by Sue Cowley

The Calm Classroom: 50 Key Techniques for Better Behaviour
The Creative Classroom: 50 Key Techniques for Imaginative
Teaching and Learning
How to Survive your First Year in Teaching, *third edition*
Getting the Buggers to Behave, *fourth edition*
Getting the Buggers into Drama
Getting the Buggers to Write, *third edition*
Getting the Buggers to Think, *second edition*
Guerilla Guide to Teaching, *second edition*
Sue Cowley's A-Z of Teaching
Sue Cowley's Teaching Clinic
Letting the Buggers be Creative
Getting your Little Darlings to Behave
The Road to Writing: A Step-By-Step Guide to Mark Making: 3-7
Teaching Skills for Dummies

The Seven E's of Reading for Pleasure

SUE COWLEY

Sue Cowley Books Ltd

2014

Sue Cowley Books Ltd
PO Box 1172
Bristol BS39 4ZJ

www.suecowley.co.uk

© Sue Cowley Books Ltd

First published 2014

Part of the 'Alphabet Sevens' Series

Also in this series:

The Seven C's of Positive Behaviour Management
The Seven P's of Brilliant Voice Usage
The Seven R's of Great Group Work
The Seven T's of Practical Differentiation

ISBN: 978-1494482381

Contents

Introduction

One of the most crucial objectives in the first few years of schooling is to ensure that children learn how to read. But as well as teaching children *how* to read, we must also find ways to help them *want* to read. Because when children enjoy reading it becomes part of their daily lives: a leisure activity they do of their own volition. And if reading is something that they want to do, then they will do it more often. As the 'Reading for Pleasure' Report from the National Literacy Trust (2006) points out: "Just because someone is able to read, does not mean that he or she will choose to do so."

A number of studies have shown how vital reading for pleasure is in ensuring high levels of literacy and in promoting future learning. Research from the OECD* has shown that reading enjoyment is more important for children's educational success than their family's socio-economic status. Researchers at the Institute of Education have recently completed a longitudinal study that demonstrates the cognitive benefits of reading for pleasure, even in apparently unrelated subjects such as maths. We know it is vital to get children reading for pleasure, and this book gives you lots of ideas about how to achieve that goal.

When we get our children 'hooked on books', we open up a world of imagination, information and ideas for them. Through a love of reading they can learn about people, places, ideas, adventures, history, geography, science, art, music, and all the many other wonders of the world. This concise guide will help all educators get their students reading for pleasure: whether you work as an early years practitioner, or as a primary, secondary or further education teacher, you will find inspiration here. This short book is packed full of ideas to help your students find pleasure in texts of all different kinds.

Reading for pleasure is not a self-indulgent exercise. Those children who choose to read every day will meet thousands of words a week. Some of these words will be old friends that they instantly recognise and understand. Others will be new words that they can incorporate into their vocabularies. Reading helps us to develop our writing skills as well, because we learn how language is constructed, and we meet correct spelling, grammar and punctuation over and over again. Reading is a form of 'play', with the reader working alongside the writer to make meaning. Those children who feel relaxed and happy around books will want to 'play with them' more often.

The latest research from the OECD shows that a growing number of children do not read for pleasure, that boys do so less than girls, and that the gap in reading for pleasure between children from different socio-economic backgrounds is widening. As educators, this research should act as an alarm call to us: warning us that we must recognise, and celebrate, the vital importance of reading for pleasure. My hope is that this book will help you encourage and build a love of reading that will stay with your children for the rest of their lives.

Sue Cowley
www.suecowley.co.uk
* OECD: Reading for Change
www.oecd.org/education/school/programmeforinternation alstudentassessmentpisa/33690986.pdf

The First E:

Early Days

The First E: Early Days

To build a love of reading, it is vital for children to be surrounded by books and reading from the earliest possible age. This makes the act of reading feel natural and pleasurable – a normal part of daily life. For many children, this happens in the home: there are lots of books around when they are tiny, and their parents or carers read to them regularly. However, for some children, the home may be completely bereft of books and of the shared experience of reading. This is where the early years setting, and later on the school, is so vital – as educators we must fill the gap for these children.

It might seem logical to wait until children can understand language before you introduce them to books. But babies can start to appreciate books, and express their choices about reading, from the very earliest days. A baby might enjoy chewing on a buggy book, rubbing her fingers over the textures of the pictures, or simply listening to the sound of mum or dad's voice. By seeing books all around, and by sharing them whenever possible, parents and educators normalise the role of books within a child's experience of the world.

To a small child, cuddling up with mum or dad or any well-loved adult to share a book is a very special experience indeed. The close physical bond and shared experience makes for an easy, relaxed atmosphere. Books come to symbolise love, happiness, security and comfort. In early years settings and schools, this relationship between parent and child is mirrored when teachers or practitioners share books with individuals, groups or with a class. The experience of being part of a community of readers is crucial for building children's long-term enjoyment of reading.

Relaxed Reading

Whatever age group you work with, make books and reading part of their daily experience, right from the word 'go'. Let them interact with texts: handling them and playing around with them and having full access to them. Make sure that your students see lots and lots of different books and texts when they are with you. Ensure that books are seen as a source of relaxation, as well as something that is there to be studied. When your students read in class, sit down and read with them, to show that this is completely normal and natural for you.

There is a lot of pressure on schools at the moment to push forwards with 'learning to read'. Synthetic phonics is an effective technique for learning how to decode sounds written on a page, and offers a quick route into early reading. However, take great care that your children do not begin to see reading only as something they *have* to do (a technical exercise) rather than as something they also *want* to do (a pleasurable one). Children are ready to learn to read at different stages in their childhood. Remember: some children will be almost a full calendar year younger than others in the same class. Children who have special educational needs may also struggle to keep up with their peers in learning to read.

In order to learn new things we have to stretch just beyond our current level of understanding or skill. The same is true of learning to read – children are not able to do it easily at first – they need to persevere and we need to be patient. Educators must take gradual steps, so that children stay relaxed and confident around books. Push too fast, and you risk the child losing interest or giving up. If you notice a child is struggling with the early stages of reading, put as much support into place as possible, as quickly as you can.

To keep things relaxed and happy on the road to reading:

✓ Allow children to play a part in choosing the books they want to read, so they get a feel for the books they like. Acknowledge that they know best what they will enjoy.

✓ Give children access to lots of great books, in lots of different situations. Visit the library regularly and have a special place for books in your teaching space. Encourage parents and carers to make space for books at home.

✓ Set aside a regular time for reading each day. For instance, reading at the end of the day in the classroom, to mirror the bedtime routine in the home. Incorporate reading for pleasure into your daily routine.

✓ Offer non-fiction choices alongside stories, and give access to texts in all different kinds of formats, including magazines, comics and electronic book readers/tablets.

✓ If you teach beginning readers, use plenty of real books alongside your phonics instruction and reading scheme books. Send real books home as well as reading scheme books.

✓ Encourage your children to use a variety of strategies to make sense of texts. A focus on synthetic phonics need not rule out the other techniques we use when we are reading. This can include sound, images, prior knowledge, sense, context, rhythm, rhyme, and so on. If a child is struggling to read using synthetic phonics alone, consider which other strategies might help.

✓ Find ways to create a feeling of success for each child. Some children respond really well to sticker charts; others prefer praise from a parent or teacher.

✓ Make sharing stories feel fun, by playing around as you read: put on voices and get the children to act out what the characters are doing.

✓ Unless you are dealing with a class set text, never insist that a child 'must' finish a book *because they have started it*. Even as an adult, I stop reading a book if I lose interest in the story, or if I feel that it is not well written.

Books for Emerging Readers

When children first learn to read independently, the level of difficulty needs to increase very gradually. This will ensure that they stay relaxed and maintain their confidence around reading. If there is too much of a gap between the child's current reading age, and the reading level required to make sense of a book, the child may get worried or frustrated. Reading scheme books are graded in order, and can be linked to the phonemes taught in class. However, reading scheme books do not have the imaginative artwork and thrilling storylines that makes books for young children so exciting to read.

Books written for children to enjoy, rather than as part of a reading scheme, use a richer and more challenging vocabulary. They have more interesting storylines and themes and the pictures are often incredibly beautiful. They often feature repeated patterns and rhythmic language, which help a story become embedded in the memory. And once that happens, a child can read and reread a book with ease. Remember, young children are not scared of words they cannot easily read, or that they do not yet understand – that is an adult 'take' on how children feel. Children will often focus on the *sound* of words as you read to them, and worry less about the meaning of each individual one. They are surprisingly adept at making sense of what they read by using the context of the story that surrounds it.

Here is a useful way to find out whether a book is at the right level for a child to read independently:

✓ Ask the child to choose a book and turn to the first page together;
✓ Get the child to read the first page out loud (or several pages if the book does not have many words);
✓ For each word that the child cannot yet read, turn down one finger;
✓ If you turn down five fingers by the end of the first page, then the book is probably too difficult for the child just at the moment;
✓ Of course, if the vocabulary is too tricky for the child to read independently, you can still read the book to the child yourself.

Relaxed Spaces for Reading

At home, there is no better place for a child to read than on a parent's lap on the sofa, or snuggled up in bed. Think about how you can mirror or echo this relaxed experience in your school or setting. Ensure that there are quiet comfy places where children can sit, relax and read. This might be in the classroom (in an early years setting/infant class) or within the wider school (in the library of a secondary school). To create relaxed spaces for reading:

✓ Consider how you can ensure comfort, for instance by offering sofas, beanbags and cushions on which the children can sit to read.
✓ Work out ways to make the space feel 'private'. Screen off your reading area so that children can read

undisturbed. At our preschool we use a net curtain rail with material hanging across it to create a private reading corner.

✓ When you are reading a story to the whole class on the carpet, have cushions available so that the children can get themselves comfy.

✓ Find spaces both inside the classroom and also outdoors for reading. When the sun shines, take your children outside to share a book under the shade of a tree.

✓ Invest in a 'Story Teller's Chair' – there are some beautiful wooden chairs available if you have a suitable outdoor space. Inside the classroom you could decorate a school chair to look magical and to be your 'Story Teller's Chair'.

✓ Buy quality bookcases, fixed or portable, or attach wire bookracks to the wall. Place these next to your private reading area.

✓ When you attach bookshelves, ensure they suit the height of the children rather than the height of the adults.

✓ Think creatively, particularly if you have the chance to design a space from scratch. Talk with your students about what they would like to see in their new reading space. How can you make private areas for children to read? For instance, you might incorporate a sunken area with cushions inside it to create a snug, secure feel.

Building Partnerships

Parents or carers are a child's first and most enduring educators. It is crucial that we let them know just how important it is to get their children reading for pleasure. Find lots of ways to encourage your children's parents and carers to support reading. Build partnerships with parents, carers and the extended family as well.

- ✓ Get parents or carers to choose a book together with their child, in the early years or primary classroom. Have a regular routine, so that the children change their reading book first thing every day, or perhaps twice a week.
- ✓ Think how you can encourage parents and children to consider their choice of book carefully, rather than just taking the first book that comes to hand. For instance, set a challenge – 'find a book you have never read before', 'choose a book that will teach you something completely new' or 'pick a book that you think will make you laugh'.
- ✓ Ask parents to add to the real books that you have on offer in your classroom by making a donation of a book from home. You could put a label in the front of each book to say who donated it.
- ✓ Ask children and parents to keep a record of the reading that they do together. This usually takes the form of a reading diary or reading log. Ask parents to 'sign off' on their child's reading and to leave a comment.
- ✓ Continue the daily reading log into secondary school as well. This might be done by English teachers or via the form tutor. Create a sense of challenge by logging the number of pages read, and having a competition between classes or forms as to who can read the most.
- ✓ Set children 'reading challenges' to do (preferably with parents), over the holiday periods. For instance, challenge them to read ten different kinds of texts together: this could include recipe books, instructions for games, quiz books, travel guides, etc.

✓ Talk about the importance of reading at home in all the different communications that you do with parents and carers. Mention how important it is in newsletters, highlight it in the school magazine, have information on your website as well.

✓ Set up book groups for staff, parents, carers and children, either mixed adult/child groups or different groups for different ages. Encourage an interest in talking about reading and books.

✓ When you give Christmas presents or end of year gifts to your children, make sure that you give books. This sends a powerful message about the value you place on reading. If you use a 'bulk buying' company such as The Book People you can get sets of books very cheaply.

Great 'Early Days' Books

There are so many great books available that it can be hard to know where to start. Of course this is a wonderful 'problem' to have, but at times you might appreciate a bit of advice. Below is a list of great books for reading to and with babies and young children, compiled with the help of parents and teachers. You could share this list with parents and carers.

If you teach older primary or secondary aged students, ask them to do a study of young children's picture books, and to make some children's books of their own. Books for young children often have a subtext that can only be discerned by the older reader. Talk with older students about how and why these children's books create that wonderful feeling of pleasure.

✓ The Snail and the Whale; Monkey Puzzle; The Gruffalo – Julia Donaldson and Axel Scheffler

- ✓ The Usborne 'That's Not My …' series (great for babies)
- ✓ The True Story of the Three Little Pigs – Jon Scieszka and Lane Smith
- ✓ Where the Wild Things Are – Maurice Sendak
- ✓ I Want my Hat Back – Jon Klassan
- ✓ The Jolly Postman; Cops and Robbers; Peepo; Each Peach Pear Plum; Bye Bye Baby; Funnybones – Janet and Allen Ahlberg
- ✓ Where's my Teddy; It's the Bear – Jez Alborough
- ✓ The Hairy Maclary stories – Lynley Dodd
- ✓ Harry and the Dinosaurs go to School – Ian Whybrow and Adrian Reynolds
- ✓ Green Eggs and Ham; Oh the Thinks you can Think! – Dr Seuss
- ✓ Who's in the Loo? – Jeanne Willis and Adrian Reynolds
- ✓ Shark in the Park – Nick Sharratt
- ✓ Pants; More Pants – Giles Andreae and Nick Sharratt
- ✓ The Blue Kangaroo Series – Emma Chichester Clark
- ✓ Click Clack Moo: Cows that Type – Doreen Cronin and Betsy Lewin
- ✓ The Charlie and Lola stories – Lauren Child
- ✓ The Winnie the Witch stories – Korky Paul
- ✓ Mixed up Fairy Tales – Hilary Robinson and Nick Sharratt
- ✓ Aliens Love Underpants – Claire Freedman and Ben Cort
- ✓ We're Going on a Bear Hunt – Michael Rosen
- ✓ So Much – Trish Cooke and Helen Oxenbury
- ✓ The Tiger Who Came to Tea – Judith Kerr
- ✓ The Little Princess stories – Tony Ross
- ✓ Sharing a Shell – Julia Donaldson and Lydia Monks
- ✓ The Very Hungry Caterpillar, Brown Bear, Brown Bear, What Do You See? – Eric Carle

The Second E:

Expertise

The Second E: Expertise

To become a great reader, and to fall in love with reading, children need to build their expertise around books, stories and language. There are many layers and levels to this expertise, and it takes time to develop. Expertise in reading means becoming an expert at decoding print – being able to identify and pronounce the words that you see written on the page easily and confidently. It also means becoming an expert at understanding how words and books work to make meaning together with their reader: gathering sense through context, rhythm, patterns, inference.

Reading Expertise

It is worth considering all the different aspects of reading expertise that a child must achieve in order to become a 'good' reader. It is easy to overlook how important the early stages are in the process of becoming a confident reader – those aspects referred to as 'book behaviours'. These early stages are vital as a building block for future confidence and success. If you work with older students who struggle with reading, you may need to focus on getting some of these book behaviours more firmly in place.

To achieve reading expertise, children need to:

- ✓ Be able to hear and identify the sounds within speech, in preparation for matching spoken sounds to those on the page. They must learn the skill of auditory discrimination – the ability to actually hear and pick out sounds.
- ✓ Build their phonemic awareness – the understanding that speech is made up of smaller units of sound (phonemes) and an ability to pick these out (to hear the

letter sounds 'd–o–g'). Building phonological awareness in the early years is vital for later confidence in reading.

✓ Understand that the words on the page of a book hold meaning, and that they can free this meaning by reading the words out.

✓ Know how to navigate a book: how to hold it the right way up and (in English) to read from back to front and follow print from left to right on the page.

✓ Learn how to look for and spot patterns within language to help them read (and write) more quickly, easily and accurately. For instance, noticing the 'tion' pattern or the use of 'ing' at the end of verbs.

✓ Understand how to draw meaning out of language and why context is important in gaining sense from a story or a piece of writing. Learn to look for meaning beyond the literal, so that they can read into and beneath what the author appears to be saying at first glance.

✓ Be able to focus and concentrate for a reasonable length of time on reading, so that their behaviour allows them to read in a relaxed and pleasurable way.

✓ Learn how to figure out what a book might be like by looking at the cover, the illustrations and the blurb. Understand from these cues and clues whether they are the right audience for this book.

✓ Decide whether they are going to enjoy a book, and want to read it, by looking at the cover, the blurb, and the first few pages.

✓ Be confident enough to take a view on what they do and do not enjoy reading and to express their own wishes and desires.

✓ For non-fiction, learn how to use a contents page and an index to get around a book, and understand how to scan a book for the information they need to find.

✓ Eventually, move from reading out loud, and 'sounding out' every word, towards reading in their heads and later on being able to skim or speed read when appropriate.

A Love of Language

People usually choose to become experts in those things that really interest them. In order to help children build a love of reading, we need first to help them build a love of language. Help them to take pleasure and delight in the way that words sound, and encourage them to play around with language to have fun. Remember: for many thousands of years we passed stories and knowledge on through oral methods. It is only relatively recently that we began to write words down, and even more recently that print books were widely available.

To help your children build a love of language:

✓ Share songs and poetry together, to build their knowledge of language and to help them learn to pick out the different sounds. Build auditory discrimination and phonological awareness to make learning to read easier.
✓ Use plenty of listening activities – for instance, listening to sound tracks, sound effects and sounds in the natural world. Build your students' listening skills by asking them to pick out the different sounds.
✓ Explore the etymology of words – examine where different words come from, and how languages change and develop over time. Encourage a sense of fascination in the spoken and written word.
✓ Share the different languages spoken by children in your setting – get them to teach you words in languages other than English. Share stories, songs and poems from other

cultures and in other languages, asking volunteers to come in to share these with your class.

✓ Share stories from the past (fairy tales, myths, legends). Show your children how we are linked to previous generations and times through the power of stories and a common oral/written history.

✓ Take a close interest in the parts and the processes of language, and build an understanding of how the different parts of language work. Discuss what an adverb does to a verb, what alliteration does to the sound of a story or poem, and so on.

✓ Build other activities *around* the joy and power of stories, for instance asking the children to take on the role of a story character, or to design their own book covers.

Parents and Carers as Experts

Your children's parents or carers are experts in their own child: they know about their child's reading habits and preferences. Why not *ask* your students' parents about their child's reading? What does their child like to read at home, and where/when are they most likely to read for pleasure? Consider how you can encourage parents to read to or with their child every night, or at least several nights a week. Certainly it is vital to explain to parents why this is important, and why it remains so even after the child has learnt to read fluently.

To help parents build their expertise and to support reading for pleasure at home:

✓ Encourage parents to join the school library, and to visit it to look for books with their children, perhaps in a weekly session or at an after school club.

- ✓ Host workshops for parents around reading related subjects, to build parental knowledge: a workshop on language development in young children, on how to teach reading through phonics, or on great story telling techniques.
- ✓ Share information with parents about the language you use around literacy. Ensure that parents know what words such as 'phoneme', 'real books', 'digraph' and so on mean by sending home a list of terminology.
- ✓ Encourage parents and carers to support their child in learning 'tricky words' (those that do not follow the usual phonic patterns). Send home a list of words with suggestions about how to help children memorise them.
- ✓ Ask for volunteers from families to come in and read with individuals or, if they are willing, to the whole class. Have an 'open door' policy when it comes to encouraging volunteers.
- ✓ Give regular 'call outs' for volunteers – parents, grandparents, older siblings. As a parent, I have found that I have to *ask* schools whether I can come in and volunteer. In my experience, we could do much more in this area.
- ✓ Set up events and competitions that boost the profile of reading both in your school or setting and at home. For instance, you could hold a competition to take a photo of a child reading in the most unusual place, with the prize of a book or an ebook reader.

Teachers as Experts

If we are going to inspire our children to become expert readers, we need to build our own expertise in reading and in books as well. Every primary teacher, and every teacher of

English at secondary level, needs to have an expert knowledge of children's literature. Every teacher of every subject should see boosting enjoyment of reading as a part of their remit.

If you are not a parent, you might not have had the opportunity to 'meet' a large number of different children's books. Talk to your librarian, or visit one of the many websites recommending books on different genres, and for different age groups. To share your reading expertise with your class:

✓ Pass on the oral stories and tales that have been handed down to you by your own family – nursery rhymes and traditional fairy stories are a key part of our oral tradition. They can form the bedrock for a later love of reading.

✓ Look for stories from the oral traditions of other cultures to share with your class, to show them the richness and diversity that stories and language can bring.

✓ Help children and parents figure out 'what to read next'. Give recommendations to them around themes, genres or authors that they might enjoy.

✓ Create a 'recommendations' display in your book area, or English classroom, and send regular reading lists home, saying: 'If you liked this book, you'll love this …'.

✓ Give students and parents lists of websites that can support reading for pleasure and help them find recommendations for their children. Try www.lovereading4kids.co.uk and www.goodreads.com as a starting point.

✓ Encourage staff to share and recommend books to each other. Have a staff notice board where ideas can be posted: 'If your class liked this … they might like this …', or 'Great books on this topic/theme are …'.

✓ Set aside time in staff meetings and on training days to share ideas about books that students will love. Think about what individual children are 'into' and how you might support these interests, especially for those students who struggle to engage with reading.

✓ Link literature from the past with that from the present. For instance, show your children how Bram Stoker's classic text *Dracula* links to vampire novels of the modern day, such as the *Twilight* series.

✓ Consult with your children and their parents, to build your expertise on the books that your school could buy to support reading for pleasure. Invest in texts that your children will choose to read, as well as those texts that you feel are 'educational' for them.

✓ Buy annual subscriptions to a wide range of magazines, consulting with your students on which ones are their favourites. Factual magazines such as 'How it Works' (published by Imagine Publishing) are brilliant for inspiring children to read for enjoyment and tend to be very popular with boys.

✓ Develop your expertise in reading related special needs, such as dyslexia. Ask whether you can go on training courses to build your knowledge. If you suspect that a child is having an issue with reading, talk with your special needs coordinator as soon as possible.

The School Librarian as Expert

If you are lucky enough to have a school librarian, he or she will be a resident expert on books, and particularly on books for children. Help your librarian to help you, by sharing your ideas, and by asking lots of questions. It is important not to assume that the students you teach are already familiar with how to use a library – for some, the first visit to the school library might be their first time in a library.

- ✓ Schools, especially secondary schools with a large library, need to have an effective 'library induction' scheme in place. The children need to be taught how to find books via a library classification system, the kinds of behaviours expected in a library environment, how to search for a book using the library IT system, and so on.
- ✓ When you take a class to the library to do research, let your librarian know ahead of time that you are coming. This gives the librarian time to gather together useful books and other texts on the topic you are studying.
- ✓ Have at least one designated 'library lesson' a week for every single class in your school.
- ✓ When you research a topic in class, ask your librarian to prepare you a box of books and other texts on and around the subject, to use in lessons.
- ✓ Set up projects together with your librarian, to encourage your children to use both the school library, and also their local library as well. For instance you might organise an author visit together, to take place in the library. If you live in a rural area, and there is a mobile library bus, set up a regular time for visits.
- ✓ Ask your librarian for recommendations for great new books that you can pass on to your young readers. As avid readers of children's literature, librarians are perfectly placed to share the best of new writing.
- ✓ Get your librarian to be closely involved in drawing up a Reading for Pleasure Policy for your school. (For more on this see 'The Fourth E: Environment'.)

Children as Experts

Encourage your children to feel that they are 'experts' in their own literacy. If they are keen on a particular genre of books, then encourage them to develop this interest by suggesting similar texts. To help your children build their expertise further:

✓ Get them to write letters to their favourite authors, to find out more about their writing. Many authors will reply to letters they receive, and this can be hugely motivating for young readers.

✓ Encourage them to see themselves as writers, as well as readers. Set lots of creative writing activities, and help them develop their writing within a favourite genre.

✓ Look for author interviews on the Internet, or in the newspapers. Keep examples when you come across them, creating an 'Author Interview' scrapbook as a reference text.

✓ Invite authors to visit your school to talk about their writing. Get the children to write questions and to 'interview' the author as though they are journalists. If you have a school magazine, your interview could feature in this.

✓ Ask your students to bring in their favourite books, and to do presentations where they recommend books to each other. They could talk about why they love a particular book, and what kind of readers might enjoy it.

✓ Encourage your students to read books to each other – this works well as a paired reading activity in class. You can also get the children reading to each other across the age groups. For instance your Year 6 students could read stories to the children in the Reception class, and your Year 11 students could read with Year 7 children.

✓ Host a 'reading for charity' event, for instance a sponsored book read with the children being sponsored according to how many pages or books they read.

✓ Set up a children's book group in your school, or encourage your children to join a local children's book group. The Federation of Children's Book Groups (www.fcbg.org.uk) is a brilliant source of information, and a vital resource for supporting children's reading groups.

✓ Encourage the children to make their own books and to 'publish' these, either by creating their own books in class, or by using a self-publishing resource such as the Scholastic 'We are Writers' scheme.

✓ The thought that they *must* finish every book they start can be enough to put some children off reading. It can also stop them from experimenting with new types of texts. Explain to your children that it is okay to read the first few pages of a book and decide that it does not 'feel right' for them.

✓ Set your children 'authentic problems' to solve through reading. For instance, ask them to work as experts in a field (environmental scientists, sports journalists) and to do research through reading different texts.

✓ Allow your students to be responsible for spending part of your budget for books. Nominate a 'book buying team' and let them decide what kind of books to buy with the money. The fact that they have chosen and bought these books themselves should act as a powerful incentive for their peers to read them.

The Third E:

Engagement

The Third E: Engagement

In order for children to feel motivated to read, they need to feel engaged by the texts they are reading. We must get across the message that reading is exciting, and entertaining, and a great way to pass the time, moving away from the idea that only certain kinds of texts are 'of value' to read. Let your children know that it is okay for them to engage with *any* kind of text: whether it is a book, a comic, a magazine, a computer game guide. The most important aspect in reading for *pleasure* is that children are reading something that *they personally* enjoy, rather than something that an adult has chosen for them.

Helping Children 'Engage'

One of the key differences between reading in the home, and reading at school, is the notion of 'choice'. When you read in your leisure time, you usually make your choice based on what you enjoy reading. This is the purest form of reading for pleasure. It is often the case in schools that it is not the students who choose what they want to read, but the teacher who chooses the text that the class will read. This is particularly so in the secondary school, where the idea of 'set texts' and 'exam texts' is very much a part of the typical English lesson.

This is not to say that we should never introduce children to new books: ones that they might not choose of their own accord. However, it does mean that we should balance the books we choose for our students with some element of choice from the students' perspective. Where a book is about a topic that the child enjoys, or is a story that they have chosen freely to read, their levels of motivation are likely to be much higher. Find out what the child is 'into' and then use every trick in the book to feed that interest. Those students who already happily read for pleasure have probably had parents or carers feeding their interests through reading from an early age.

Here are some tips for helping your children to engage with all kinds of texts:

✓ Ask your children which topics or genres they enjoy and make an effort to go out and source books on these areas. Ensure that children have access to these texts via a school library or a class book loan system.

✓ Offer an element of choice in reading by asking your students to vote on what book they would like to hear at storytime. Before you pick a reading book, offer the students three options and then pick the one that most prefer.

✓ If you are an early years practitioner working with babies, here is a great way to offer them a choice of books. Give your babies a couple of books to look at, and then when they drop one book, read the other one with them.

✓ When you are going to read a book to your class, read it through yourself first so that you are comfortable and confident with the text. That way you can relax and help your children engage with it. The more familiar the text is to you, the more experimental you can be with the style in which you read it.

✓ Read some books that are full of pace and excitement – that have a strong entertainment factor. Talk with your children to find out which subjects they find exciting and entertaining.

✓ Encourage your children to think about what a book might be about by looking at its cover. What genre do they think it will be? Will there be danger and dramatic tension in the story? Which book would they choose based on the cover alone?

✓ Hide the covers of some of the books that you have in class, and encourage your children to 'take a chance on a mystery book'. A sense of mystery and curiosity is very engaging for children.

✓ Develop this idea even further, perhaps in your library, by having a whole shelf of 'mystery' books with their spines facing inwards. Do your children dare to take a chance on a 'mystery' story?

✓ Introduce your children to series books, reading the first book in class, and then encouraging the children to read the rest of the series outside school. That feeling of wanting to know 'what happens next?' is great for encouraging children to read.

✓ When you are reading a longer book to your class, stop reading at the point in the story where there is a 'cliffhanger'. This ensures that your children are keen to hear the rest of the story.

✓ When you read class novels together, involve your children by asking them to take on characters within the story. Get individual students to read the words of dialogue that each character says. This is a fun way to share the reading around the class.

✓ When you are studying a 'difficult' text with your class, use every strategy possible to make it feel engaging and relevant. Extracts, film, dramatisations, links to modern day texts: all these can help your students see how a story from the past is relevant to their lives today.

Keeping a Focus

When you use 'reading for pleasure' as a whole class or whole school activity, there is always the possibility that some children appear to be reading but are actually doing little or no reading at all. There is an element of trust at work here: do you have faith that your students will do what you ask them to? Much depends on the relationship that you have with your children and on your knowledge about them as individuals. Remember that when they see their teacher 'reading for pleasure' alongside them, this sends a very powerful message about your views on reading. Where the whole school is reading together at the same time, including *all* the adults, this sends a very strong message about the value of reading.

If you are concerned that your children might not all be focused on their reading, here are some strategies to help them keep a focus:

✓ Ask your children to give feedback after a silent reading session, for instance retelling the story to a partner or explaining three things they found out in a non-fiction text.

✓ Sit with individuals while the class is doing silent reading to listen to them read. Identify their areas of weakness, giving additional support to build reading skills.

✓ Ask your children to work in pairs, taking it in turns for one person to read a paragraph or a page to the other.

✓ Add some fun to private reading by using a 'speed dating' approach. Half the class choose a book to read, the other children visit each reader for a few minutes, one after the other. During their 'date' the reader must read as well as possible to their dating partner. At the end, ask the students which book they would choose to 'date' and why.

Interacting with Books

Modern children live in a highly interactive world – the Internet, touch screen technology, virtual reality, computer games, ebook readers, tablets – interactivity has become an integral part of their lives. Reading a book is all about interacting with its author – without a reader the book lies inert on the shelf. The more we encourage children to *want* to interact with books, the more likely they are to develop a passion for reading.

Here are some ideas for boosting interactivity:

- ✓ Offer big or huge books as an option for reading. Oversized books are exciting for young readers and very large books seem especially appealing to boys. Remember, the bigger the book, the larger the illustrations will be. The outsized *Dinosaurs* book by Steve Brusatte (Quercus, 2008) is a teenage/adult level book that is hugely engaging because of the enormous size of its dinosaur illustrations.
- ✓ With the youngest children, use some 'big book' versions of popular children's stories to share with your class. This catches the children's attention and ensures that everyone can enjoy the illustrations.
- ✓ Buy a 'class ebook reader' and ask your students what books they would like you to download onto it. Have a rota system so that everyone gets a chance to read ebooks as well as paper based texts.
- ✓ Books that include interesting textures are great for engagement and interactivity. The Usborne 'That's not my …' series is brilliant for reading with babies and very

young children. The multi-sensory textures in the books really encourage children to interact with them in a physical way.

✓ Pop-up books are great for capturing your children's imagination. For instance, the pop-up version of Michael Rosen's 'We're Going on a Bear Hunt' includes lots of pieces to slide and move as you say the words. The 'Encyclopedia Prehistorica Dinosaurs' by Robert Sabuda and Matthew Reinhert is a stunning work of paper engineering.

✓ Get your children to interact with the stories they hear by being active participants in the story telling. Invite them to join in with repeated phrases, or to act out the actions that the characters are doing.

✓ Books such as 'The Jolly Postman' encourage interactivity through the little cards and letters that the children can take out to read. The miniature nature of these features is very appealing to children.

✓ Electronic book readers such as the 'Leadpad' are great for encouraging interactive reading. You can also find lots of interactive book Apps for tablets to use with your children.

Writing for Pleasure

Writing is, of course, the flipside of reading. One of the most useful methods I have found of encouraging my own children to read for pleasure is to write for them and with them. I grasp every opportunity that I can find for us to create *our own* texts. This technique would work brilliantly in the classroom as well, especially given how simple it is now to publish your own books. By going through the processes of plotting, writing, editing, proof reading, cover design and so on, you give a brilliant example to the children about what being 'an author' involves. You might:

- ✓ Write a story together as a whole class for publication in a school magazine or online. Once you have devised a plot together, get individuals or small groups to write one paragraph of the story each.
- ✓ If you need a piece of text for a particular purpose in class, write it yourself. This allows you to create a piece of text that is tailored to the learning objective you have in mind. For instance, you can write a piece that shows a specific kind of error and ask the children to spot the mistakes and undo them.
- ✓ When your children sit down to do writing, sit down and do it with them, and share the end results that you achieve. This sends a useful message about how much pleasure you get out of writing for others to read.
- ✓ If you have old exercise books, stories or essays that you wrote when you were younger, be brave and share them with your students. Show them that all writers develop over time.
- ✓ Create a class blog and upload your pieces of writing for other people (especially parents and carers) to read for pleasure.
- ✓ Set up a school magazine together with your children. This offers a wonderful opportunity for them to see their work in print, and to have it published to an audience of friends and family.

The Fourth E:

Environment

The Fourth E: Environment

A key part of an educator's skill is to create an environment in which children can learn effectively. Consider all the ways that you can create an environment in which reading is clearly signalled as 'pleasurable'. Think about what this means both for your teaching space, and also across your school or setting as a whole. Consider how you can model the idea of reading for pleasure for your students through your use of the space. Think too about how resources can trigger positive associations for your children.

Research has shown that children come to reading much earlier and easier, and tend to find it more pleasurable, when they have grown up in a 'print rich' and 'language rich' environment. In a home where there are lots of books and other texts, children see reading as a normal part of life. In a home where there are plenty of conversations with caregivers, children become comfortable and confident about using language.

In a twenty-year long study at the University of Nevada, researchers discovered something amazing: having lots of books in the home has an incredibly powerful effect on the level of education that a child will attain. The number of books in the home has a more powerful effect than the level of education of a child's parents and various other factors, including parental income. You can find out more about the research here: www.eurekalert.org/pub_releases/2010-05/uonr-bih052010.php.

Encourage your children to take books home from the school library every week, and to take several books for holiday periods. Ensure that even those children who do not live in a book rich environment have access to books when they are not at school. Actively encourage your children to bring in books and other texts from home, to show, share and read with others. Help all your students to have access to the wonderful gift of language, by creating a 'text rich' and 'language rich' environment in your setting or school.

- ✓ Posters typically use vivid and eye catching text and graphics. Display a great array of posters, including those in languages other than English. Change your posters regularly, for instance to tie in with a new topic. Have a 'Welcome' poster on your door or in your entrance area, which says 'welcome' in a variety of languages.
- ✓ Create a reading area where your children can go to spend time with books and other kinds of texts. Ensure that this is private, welcoming and comfy, and also that you allow time for the children to use it. If possible, allow them to access this area both before and after the school day.
- ✓ Have a 'topic table' on which you display resources around a class topic. Include different examples of texts on your topic table, and encourage your children to bring in texts (ready made or self created) to add to the display.
- ✓ Take care that your environment does not become too 'busy', with too many different examples of text, as this can prove distracting. At a quiet moment, step outside your teaching space and then enter it as though you are completely new to it. What strikes you first? Does it feel busy or confusing? Would you be able to relax and read for pleasure in this space?
- ✓ Set up a holiday reading scheme, so that your school becomes a place to read for pleasure outside of term time. Motivate and engage the students who attend by choosing themes that really excite them. For instance,

linking up with a local football club for a week of sports related reading, topped off by a 'behind the scenes' tour of the football ground.

Developing Displays

Displays are great for highlighting the status of reading for pleasure within your setting, in the classroom and around the building. Encourage staff and students to contribute to displays on reading, and refresh your displays regularly. Make sure that displays are fixed at the right height for your children to read them. As adults, it is all too easy to put them up at your own eye level, rather than at that of your students.

✓ Have lots of 'reading recommendations' displays, so that staff and students can share their favourite books with each other. You might recommend books around a theme, books for a particular age group, books within a genre, and so on.

✓ Experiment with setting up trails, and treasure hunts, and puzzles, to encourage your children to interact with your displays. For instance, you might post quotes from different books around the school, and have a competition to see who can identify the books that they come from.

✓ Create a 'Reading Tree' display for a shared space, for instance in your Reception area or Assembly Hall. Give out leaf shapes to your students, and ask them to write about a recommended book on their leaf. Add the leaves to your 'Reading Tree'. Encourage parents to add their own recommendations, for instance when they come into school for a Consultation Evening.

✓ Develop some 'take away' displays, where students can interact with the display and take something away from it. For instance, in the 'Reading Tree' example above, peg rather than stick the leaves to the tree, to let children take recommendations away with them.

✓ Base displays around a theme, with key phrases that might be found in books of that genre. For instance, you could have a 'Once upon a time ...' and 'They all lived happily ever after ...' display about fairytales.

✓ Photocopy the book covers of your children's favourite books, and ask the students to add speech bubble commentaries. Their commentary could explain what happens in the story, what the book is like and why someone should read it.

✓ Create an 'Author of the Month' display. This is especially useful if you have an author visit planned, as you can link the visit to a display recommending the author's books. Show the author your display when he or she visits, and get some authentic comments or quotes to add to your display.

✓ Think laterally about surfaces for displays. One of the most striking text displays I have ever seen was in a classroom where the walls were in need of redecoration. The teacher had asked for permission to paint directly onto the walls. She and her students had painted a black backdrop for their topic of war poetry. The graphic nature of the design, and the fact that it was 'permanent' made it feel very powerful.

✓ Ceilings make an unusual place for displays. Use 'washing line' style displays that hang across your teaching space. For a 'secret reading display', use the underside of desks and let your children hide underneath to read what is there.

Furniture

Think carefully about how you display the different kinds of books and texts that you have in your classroom, and in your school library. Ideally, you want them to be easily accessible, and visible. Think about where the children sit to read, and how the furniture you have encourages them to relax and feel comfortable. Ensure that you:

✓ Have at least one bookrack on which you can display books with the covers facing outwards. Let the children see the covers of the books easily, to help them make a choice about which ones to read.
✓ Put your bookcases at child, rather than adult, height. For instance, if you have a wire rack bookcase on your wall, check that it is at the right level for your children to access it.
✓ In the library, have bookracks with 'themed' or 'recommended' books on display, to encourage children to try new genres or to read widely within a favourite genre. Ask the students to set up genre displays of their own, selecting books that they know their peers would love to read.
✓ Have some furniture that allows your books to be portable. For instance, you can buy book boxes on wheels that you can move around your setting, and take outside whenever the weather allows.
✓ Where possible within the confines of your space and budget, offer cosy and comfy furniture on which children can sit and read – sofas, beanbags, cushions, rugs, and so on. Let the children read sitting on a window ledge or laying on the carpet.

✓ Consider how you can screen off your reading area, so that it feels secretive and private. For instance, you could use a rail with material strung across it, or moveable wooden screens.

Resources

Incorporate real life resources into your teaching to bring the children's reading to life. Resources can lift the words of a book from the page, and they help children to build their imagination and to think creatively. Resources can help kindle a sense of curiosity, so that your students really want to find out more through reading. You might inspire reading for pleasure by sharing:

✓ Historical artefacts, such as coins, pottery or authentic looking weapons, when reading a Horrible Histories book;
✓ Examples of costumes that the characters in the story you are reading would wear, for instance dressing up as a story character to host a 'reading for pleasure' assembly;
✓ Food and drink, linked to the reading you are doing, for instance cooking Victorian gruel while reading 'Oliver Twist' by Charles Dickens;
✓ Natural resources, such as pine cones, seeds, sticks, plants, to inspire reading for research into the natural world;
✓ In the early years or primary classroom, you could set up your role play area as a 'book shop' or as a 'library'.

The Whole School Environment

Ensure that the environment right across your setting reflects the importance that you place on reading for pleasure. Think laterally about where displays can go, considering spaces both inside and outside the building. Put displays in unusual places, such as the toilets, the changing rooms, the canteen or hanging from the ceilings – wherever they are likely to catch your students' attention.

As part of your commitment to reading for pleasure, develop a Reading for Pleasure Policy to underline the importance you place on reading for pleasure. As with any kind of policy document, it is very important that this is not just something written on paper, but that it is a living, breathing, ever evolving outline of your vision.

Think about the kind of language you use within your policy. Does the way you express your vision make a clear and firm statement about how vital you believe it is for children to read for pleasure? Use a team approach to develop your policy, encouraging all staff to contribute, so that they are more likely to take ownership of what is written. Encourage your librarian to play a key role in developing the policy, and ensure that it has the full backing of your head teacher, preferably working in a 'hands on' role during the development phase.

Here are some useful questions for thinking about what should go into a 'Reading for Pleasure Policy':

✓ Who is your policy for and why does your setting feel it is important for children and adults to read for pleasure?
✓ How can you ensure access and equality for all in reading for pleasure?
✓ Have you included references to texts from other cultures, and in other languages?
✓ How can you support children with special educational needs and/or disabilities in reading for pleasure? How

will you use special technologies to help children access texts?

✓ What different kinds of text might be read for pleasure in your school or setting and how will you check that all these kinds of texts are available?

✓ What role would you like different members of staff to take in encouraging children to read for pleasure?

✓ How will your policy work across the curriculum – what role do you want teachers of subjects other than English to play?

✓ How will you link with and support families in helping their children to want to read for pleasure?

✓ How would you describe your commitment to your library as a key resource in children reading for pleasure? How can you support wider access to your library including during breaks, before and after school and outside of term times?

✓ What role does your local (non-school) library have to play in your policy? How will you develop links to ensure that all children have access to books outside school?

✓ What kind of budget will you provide to support activities around reading for pleasure, and who will be in charge of this budget?

✓ What commitment will you make to training and continuing professional development to support your work in this area?

✓ How you will evaluate your policy and its effectiveness, and adapt it on an ongoing basis?

The Fifth E:

Emotions

The Fifth E: Emotions

Reading is very much an emotional as well as an intellectual act. We talk of 'losing ourselves' in a book. Readers cry tears of genuine sadness at a tragic book, or laugh out loud at a funny one. The best stories help us feel empathy with the characters within them. We will say to a friend, 'you simply *must* read this' when we finish a brilliant book. Show your children how stories can stir their emotions, and find books that encourage a sense of interest and involvement from your students.

When we choose to do something 'for pleasure', it stands to reason that we are likely to do more of it. The emotional gratification that we get from reading feeds into us wanting to do it more frequently. As we do more of it, it becomes easier; as it gets easier, we can do more of it more easily. Research has repeatedly shown that reading motivation tends to decrease with age: as children move to secondary school their motivation often drops. Boys are also generally less motivated to read for pleasure than girls (National Literacy Trust, 2006). Wherever possible, it is vital for us to get children hooked on reading while they are young: it is that much harder to build motivation and confidence later on.

Reading Role Models

Studies have shown that, where parents themselves believe that reading is pleasurable, this improves children's motivation and reading achievement. Those parents who enjoy reading will model 'reading for pleasure' all the time for their children. The teacher is also vital as a reading role model, especially for those children who do not have parents or carers to model this attitude. Ask yourself how often your students see you reading for pleasure. Encourage your children to share their love of reading with at least one family member or friend, so that they feel they are part of a 'reading community'. If their parents do not enjoy reading, can they bond with a grandparent or a cousin or a friend to share a love of books?

Sometimes educators and parents focus on children finding 'suitable reading matter', whereas when children talk about reading for pleasure, they report reading comics, magazines, websites or jokes. Be conscious of how your own views on what is 'suitable' or 'of value' can subconsciously filter through to your students. Remember that you are modelling attitudes, as well as actions and activities. To boost the profile of reading role models:

✓ Host an assembly where teachers and other staff talk about why, what and where they read for pleasure. Encourage your children to see reading as a leisure activity that adults actively choose to do.

✓ Contact local celebrities or past students and ask them if they would come in to talk to the children about the role of reading in their lives.

✓ When you set a reading activity in class, read alongside your students. If you have a regular 'private reading' session, bring in your own book and read for pleasure at the same time as your children. Do not always feel that you must be moving around the classroom checking up on them. The act of modelling what you want your children to do can send a far more powerful message than time spent telling them to 'get on with your reading'.

- ✓ Set up events to encourage fathers to read more with their sons and daughters. (See 'Get your Boys Reading' in the final part of this book for more ideas.)
- ✓ Talk to your children about what books mean to you: if you are passionate about reading this will filter through in subconscious as well as conscious ways. Talk about how you read as a child and what books meant to you when you were young.

The Motivation to Read

It is tricky to boost students' motivation, because motivation is such a complex and personal thing. Some children are motivated best by challenges, others love to be rewarded, while others have a thirst for knowledge that they want to quench. Student choice is a key strategy to increase motivation. If children have an element of choice in their reading this increases their motivation to get through any difficulties involved in making sense of a text.

To boost motivation in your class or school:

- ✓ Celebrate progress to boost confidence, for instance giving a special reading sticker for every three, or five, or seven nights of reading signed off by a parent or carer.
- ✓ Create a challenge for your students, for example asking them to 'read a pile of books as tall as yourself' over the course of the school year. Get the students to create a 'book height chart'. As they read each one, they can measure the spine and draw it on their chart, labelled with the name of the book.
- ✓ Ask your students about their interests – which subjects really grab their attention outside of school? Which topics do they want to find out more about? Base some of your planning on the information that they give you.

✓ Find out about your children's hobbies outside school, and find texts around these subjects to share with your class. A hobby is something that we do out of choice, in our own free time, so we are well motivated to do it.

✓ Explore ways to develop intrinsic reading motivation. Ideally your students should want to read because it gives them pleasure, rather than because of external rewards. Find ways to boost attitudes such as curiosity, involvement, excitement and fascination. When you hold a competition, make books the prize.

✓ At secondary level you can still offer an element of student choice about the books studied in English lessons. For instance, giving students a choice from a variety of 'themes', encompassing different texts, taught by different teachers within an English department. You can see an example of how this could work in 'You Choose' here http://edutronic.net/you-choose/.

✓ Find some stories that have characters with which your children can readily empathise: people in similar situations, characters with similar emotions, or of a similar age to your readers. For instance you could read 'Harry and the Dinosaurs go to School' with your Reception class to explore their feelings about starting school.

✓ Where you teach texts that are not so easy for children to identify with, draw out the parallels for and with them. Show them how and why there are connections between their lives and the lives of the people in these books.

✓ Find non-fiction texts that inspire curiosity, and that break down complex ideas to a level where children can access them. If a book gives too much information, this can be off-putting to a child; equally if a book is too simplistic, this may diminish the pleasure that the child gets out of it. Offer various texts on the same non-fiction topic, so that your students have a choice about which one best suits their current reading level.

Finding the Fun in Reading

Reading is essentially a form of 'play': especially the reading of fiction. When we read a story, we play within the imaginative world that the author has created for us. Through this 'play', reading helps us to develop our understanding of different contexts, different people, and different social situations. There are many ways that you can help your children see reading as 'fun'. Here are some ideas:

✓ When you read picture books to your class, hold the book facing the children (you will need to learn the knack of reading upside down). The illustrations are a huge part of the fun of a story so let the children see and enjoy them.

✓ Encourage your children to sit in a relaxed way when you share stories, and when they do private reading. If your children feel physically relaxed, they are more likely to enjoy the book they are reading. This is not the time to insist on 'sitting properly'.

✓ Effective classroom management is important for a sense of 'fun'. The children need to feel certain that you can manage the behaviour of the group so that they can read (or hear you read) without interruption. They should also feel safe to say that they love reading, without worrying that their peers might be dismissive of this.

✓ Supplement the books at your setting with books of your own. This demonstrates to your children just how much you love reading and also how much you care about them. There is something immensely powerful about a teacher bringing in one of his or her own books, to give to an individual child, and saying 'I read this and thought of you'. This does not have to be expensive – trawl your local charity shops for great value second hand books.

✓ Be relaxed enough to pause and chat about a book or story as you read it. What do the children think? Can they give their ideas? What do they think happens next? Would they like to make up some actions to go with the story? Play around with the ideas in the text as you read.

The Teacher as Reader

The way that the teacher reads to his or her class has a powerful impact on how the children feel about the story, and about reading more generally. As a teacher you must become an expert at reading out loud, and at doing so in such a way that the children feel drawn to listen to you. Help your students understand that reading is fun by making it *sound* fun as you do it. You can:

✓ Play around with the voices of the characters as you read, varying the tone of your voice to bring the people within a story to life.

✓ Vary the pace at which you read to build a sense of dramatic tension, or to enhance the sound of the language. Where the writer uses alliteration, use your voice to 'pick out' the sounds so that the children hear how this technique works. Read slowly, then quickly, imagining the words as chewing gum that can be stretched and modulated.

✓ Let your personal enthusiasm for reading come through in the way you read to your children. Your students will be able to sense whether or not you are enjoying yourself, by listening to whether your voice sounds relaxed and happy. Read with a 'smile' in your voice.

✓ Put emphasis on key words, and slow down where the words might be tricky for the children to understand. Talk about the words that the author uses to help your children learn new vocabulary.

✓ Remember the children will be looking at your face when you read. Your facial expressions can enhance the expressiveness of your reading. When you look curious as you read, you will create a curious tone in your voice.

✓ Sometimes, read out loud to your class from the back of your classroom. Ask the students to close their eyes and listen, rather than looking at you as you read. This gives a lovely relaxed feeling to the reading.

The Sixth E:

Experiences

The Sixth E: Experiences

Encourage your young readers to see themselves as epic adventurers, on the brink of an amazing journey of discovery. Through a love of reading, they can discover anything and everything that they want to know about the world in which they live. That feeling of curiosity, of desperately wanting to know what is out there, is one of the keys to reading for pleasure. An intense desire to find out more about your world is a powerful motivation to read. Reading unlocks knowledge for the curious child: as educators we must feed and build on that innate sense of curiosity. We need children to *want* to answer the questions: who, what, where, when, why and how?

Inspire and motivate your readers to want to find out more about the world in which they live, by linking the reading they do to real life experiences. This might involve going on exciting trips and visits, or setting up events. You can also build 'real life style' experiences for them within your setting or school – dramatised representations of a part of real life that cannot be offered as a direct experience. For instance, your children could imagine that they are exploring the rainforest, or that they are astronauts flying through space. What can they find out as they journey through these places? The power of real or imagined experience helps children see the value and purpose of reading. We want them to believe that, if they have a keen interest in a particular topic, the obvious next step is to find out more about it through reading.

Trips

There is something truly magical for children (and hopefully for their teachers as well) about going on a trip somewhere outside school. For some children, a school trip gives access to something far beyond their normal experiences of the world. Going on a trip can bring a subject or topic to life, lifting it off the pages of the book and into the real world of experiences. To build reading for pleasure through school trips:

✓ Learn more about a topic, place or subject before your trip by reading for research. Study a map to put the place you are visiting into its geographical context, or read more about the history of a building you are going to explore.

✓ Use storybooks before your trip to build up a sense of anticipation. Read a story about a fire or a fire fighter, before a visit to the local fire station, or a story about wild animals before you visit a wildlife park.

✓ After your trip, use the experience to motivate writing, as well as reading, for pleasure. Share what you have discovered by writing about it, and share your texts with other classes, with parents, with everyone.

✓ Encourage your students to choose one aspect of your trip, and to read more deeply into this area. For instance, if you go on a trip to the theatre, some children might read to feed an interest in set design, while others might read to find out more about how special effects are created on stage.

✓ Some trips are perfect for boosting enjoyment of reading, because they are all about enjoying reading. There are a number of children's book festivals you can visit, for instance Bath Festival of Children's Literature (www.bathfestivals.org.uk/childrens-literature/).

Visitors

Invite visitors into your school or setting to bring the learning to life, and to encourage the children to build their interest in a particular topic or subject. A fascinating visitor can help your children discover an interest in a new topic. Surround any visits with chances to read lots of different texts on the topic in question. For instance:

- ✓ You organise a visit from a rainforest adventure group, who bring in tropical spiders, reptiles and other creatures. During the visit, the children act as jungle explorers and imagine they are travelling through a jungle. Afterwards, you share related books, including the Steve Backshall 'Deadly Sixty' books (factual animal books) and storybooks featuring Dora the Explorer and her cousin Diego, an animal rescuer working in the rainforest.
- ✓ You arrange for a local birds of prey group to bring some birds into your setting. The birds include a variety of owls, which the children are encouraged to hold. Afterwards you share factual books on birds of prey and read the story 'The Owl who was Afraid of the Dark'. You create a pamphlet giving information about the different kinds of birds.
- ✓ You organise an author visit and workshop for the students. (If you have a school librarian, ask for help to arrange this – children's authors are keen to build links with schools, as this gives them direct contact with their audience.) The children interview the author and do a write up for the school magazine or website. The author leaves the school a set of signed copies of his/her books,

and the children take it in turns to borrow these to read at home.

Imaginary Experiences

It is often the case that the knowledge we want our children to learn about is not actually available in the 'real world'. This is where stories and imaginary experiences have great power. We cannot transport our children back millions of years to experience dinosaurs at first hand, or take them to a live dig just at the moment when a fossil is found. But we can ask them to imagine they are palaeontologists digging up a dinosaur skeleton and get them to read more about what they have 'discovered'.

You can set up 'provocations' for your children, as part of a varied diet of imaginary experiences. A provocation is a situation designed to inspire or provoke a response from them. For instance, when the students arrive at the classroom they discover a locked treasure chest. What could be inside? Who could have left it? And should they open it? Perhaps it is a pirate's treasure? This could inspire you to read all sorts of books and stories about pirates.

Or you could take them out in the playground and show them an animal that has got itself trapped in a tree. Can they work as 'animal rescuers' and figure out a way to get the animal down? They will need to do some reading first, to find out what kind of animal it is and whether it is dangerous. Or you could black out the windows of your classroom and ask your students to imagine that you are spending the night in a haunted house. Then you could read some books with torches, with spooky sound effects playing in the background.

Events

Although it takes a lot of organisation, a one-off or regular event provides a fantastic focus for promoting an enjoyment of reading. It helps to build the sense that your school or setting is made up of a 'community of readers'. You could:

✓ Set up a book club or book group in which students talk together about a book they have read and enjoyed. This might be run as a lunch or after school club, perhaps just for students, or maybe with parents/carers and staff joining in as well.

✓ Host an 'All Read Together' day, where you invite parents and carers in to spend time reading with the children. You could focus your day on encouraging fathers to read with their children, or on getting grandparents to become reading volunteers.

✓ Put on a Shakespeare Day/Festival, when teachers and students dress up as characters from Shakespeare's plays. You could hold a special assembly at which groups act out scenes and read Shakespearean sonnets.

✓ Join in with the annual Children's Book Week – an event that has been running for over 80 years. During the week, teachers and children dress up as characters from children's literature, share stories, explore libraries and local bookshops, and do lots of story telling and story writing. Visit www.booktrust.org.uk.

✓ Take part in a book award 'shadowing' process, where you read the books that have been nominated for an award. For instance 'Carnegie Shadowing', see www.carnegiegreenaway.org.uk/shadowingsite/.

Challenges

Children respond really well to a challenge: students love to compete against others, either individually or as part of a group. They also love competing against themselves, and against their teachers. You could challenge your students to:

✓ Read a pile of books as tall as themselves over the course of the school year, and take a photograph to prove it. Encourage staff to join in with this challenge as well by building 'reading towers' in your staffroom.

✓ Read a mountain of books – who can reach the top of the mountain first? You could set different height mountains for students of different ages.

✓ See which class or form group can read the most words during a whole school reading session, or which group can 'guess the book' from a series of quotes or extracts.

✓ Go on a 'text hunt' in groups around the school, piecing all the bits of text together to find a paragraph from a well-known story. The first group to find the book in the library are the winners.

✓ Take part in a 'Big Book Swap' where everyone is invited to bring one book into school, and to swap it for a book that someone else has brought in. You could provide books from a local charity shop, or old books that you no longer use, for any children who do not have books of their own.

✓ Hold competitions in areas related to reading, for instance to design a book mark or to create a new cover design for your school brochure.

The Seventh E:

Everyone, Everwhere, Everything

The Seventh E: Everyone, Everywhere, Everything

Ideally, we want to get *everyone* reading, *everywhere* that they can, and *everything* that is available to read (within age appropriate limits obviously). Find ways to make it feel like reading can be done anywhere at all within your setting and beyond. Ask your students to have a favourite reading book in their bag at all times, and encourage them to pull it out for a quick read whenever they have a moment. This might be in the lunch queue, or at the end of a lesson if they have finished their work. Set up a scheme whereby members of staff are encouraged to 'catch a child reading'. You might have a special badge that says: 'I got caught reading' to hand out to students. (You can get custom made badges on the auction site www.ebay.co.uk.)

Everyone Reads

It is a great idea to set aside a regular time and space during each day or week when all children choose a book and read it. In the secondary school this might be in tutor time, or in English lessons. For the early years setting or primary school this could be first thing every morning. One great approach is to get *everyone* in the school to stop what they are doing and read for pleasure, including all the staff. This really boosts the status of reading as a pleasurable activity.

To give a boost to your 'everyone reads' scheme, find a catchy title. Here are some past and present favourites:

- ✓ ERIC – Everyone Reads In Class;
- ✓ USSR – Uninterrupted Sustained Silent Reading;
- ✓ DEAR – Drop Everything And Read.

You could also devise an acronym of your own (or get your students to make one up). Incorporate some humour to catch your students' attention. For instance:

- ✓ WART – We All Read Together; or perhaps
- ✓ RAT – Reading All Together; but probably not
- ✓ FART – Focus And Read Together. (Although I am sure this would be extremely popular with your boys).

By encouraging your children to feel that they are part of a larger group of people who all read – a reading community – you make reading for pleasure feel like a natural part of life. When all the children in your setting read, get all the adults to join in as well.

Parents who regularly read a book or a newspaper in their children's presence are sending an incredibly strong message about the status of reading in their lives. However, even the most supportive of parents will often stop reading to or with their children once their children can read independently. Let parents know that it is still really important to share texts and books with their children, even after they can read independently. Or to put it another way, we should not punish our children for learning to read by no longer reading with them.

Routines for Reading

Some children come from a home where there are very few routines in place. They have chaotic home lives, without anyone who can or will read regularly to them. Create routines around reading, so that it becomes one of the 'good habits' that you encourage. Give your children the sense of structure that might be missing at home. Incorporate some or all of the following activities into your day-to-day routines:

✓ Listen regularly to your children reading, and ask for volunteers to come in and hear the children read on a regular basis. If your children are confident readers, get them reading in groups, so that everyone gets a chance to read to other people, and to hear other readers.

✓ Read aloud to your class, sometimes with a specific learning focus, but sometimes simply for the sheer pleasure of hearing a story. *Even at secondary school.*

✓ Have a regular time when 'everyone reads', as part of your class or whole school routine. Consider the best time of the day or week for this to happen.

✓ Give your students a reading log or reading diary, and reward those who fill this out regularly.

Guided Reading

'Guided Reading' is a carousel style teaching approach in which the teacher works on reading with one small group at a time, for around twenty minutes a day. The children talk about and analyse a book or text, read out parts of it, and generally work alongside the teacher to draw meaning from it. This approach is useful for helping children develop the skills of inference and prediction, and to think about how the author matches his or her style to the reader. It is also helpful for showing children how to 'get more' out of what they read, i.e. how to dig deeper into the ways that an author shapes a piece of text for the reader's pleasure.

When using guided reading:

✓ Consider the best time of day for this – avoid times that are likely to be disrupted by 'admin' type tasks (for instance, directly after play or lunchtime when you may be dealing with children's disputes). Pick a time when the children will not be too tired to focus and concentrate.

✓ Think carefully about what the other students will do while you focus on the guided reading group. Set clear targets and roles for the other children within the class so that they are more likely to stay on task.

✓ Consider using a 'book club' style model – where the children discuss the kind of books they like and why they like reading them, rather than an overtly analytical approach.

✓ Use your guided reading sessions to build reading skills, for instance supporting children who are struggling with their reading by developing their knowledge of phonics.

✓ Balance the 'analysis style' approach of guided reading with times when you read to and with the children for pure pleasure, with no emphasis at all on analysing what they are reading.

Get your Boys Reading

Research has found that boys are less likely to read for pleasure, and also that they are less likely to read on a regular or daily basis. The suggestions below will help you encourage your boys to see reading as pleasurable. (These points are intended to be general ones about how boys typically respond to different kinds of reading, so please excuse any elements of stereotyping involved.)

To encourage your boys to read:

✓ Put non-fiction texts on a par with fiction ones. Although story time is great for building a love of reading, many boys actually prefer to read non-fiction texts. Teachers typically choose a storybook when reading to the whole class. Remember to include non-fiction books as part of your diet of whole class reading sessions.

✓ Add an element of mystery to the act of reading, by offering your children some 'do you dare to read?' challenges. Wrap scary books up in a plain brown cover or a black bin bag and dare your boys (and girls) to see who is brave enough to read them.

✓ Introduce your boys to series books: boys really enjoy the challenge of reading all the books in a series. There are many brilliant series books available for boys, often in genres such as adventure, action and horror. The 'Beast Quest' books and Darren Shan's various series are great for engaging boys.

✓ Identify a 'need' that your boys have then find the right kind of books to fulfil that need. For instance, many boys love computer games, so the 'Prima Games Guides' really appeal to them. These books explain how to work your way through the different levels in Nintendo DS, Wii and other computer games. Boys love the notion that a book will help them figure out how to succeed in a favourite computer game.

✓ Find books that reflect what boys aspire to be and to do – ones that have characters who can act as role models for your students, or ones that feature situations that your children will find exciting. Playing football, exploring a jungle, working as a palaeontologist, sailing the oceans, battling aliens – whatever your boys enjoy.

✓ Boys often respond really well to books that give extreme examples – the biggest, the tallest, the deadliest, the fastest, and so on. Try 'The Guinness Book of Records' or Steve Backshall's 'Deadly Sixty' books.

- ✓ Boys love books that make them laugh so use humorous books and texts, alongside serious ones. Find books that include jokes, ones that use toilet humour and ones that have a gross or disgusting subject matter. The Horrible Histories series and the Horrible Science books are very popular with boys. Try Mitchell Symons' 'How Much Poo Does an Elephant Do?' for gross facts.
- ✓ Use favourite topics or hobbies that your boys have as a focus for reading. For instance, the 'Reading the Game' scheme (see www.readingthegame.org.uk) offers resources around the ever-popular football theme.
- ✓ Show your boys that their love of action and adventure can be fed by books, as well as by films. Use film to introduce boys to some great book series, such as Harry Potter, the Diary of a Wimpy Kid or the Percy Jackson books.
- ✓ Find role models for your boys, particularly male role models who love to read. Ask fathers and grandfathers to come in and read with your children to show them that men love reading too.
- ✓ Get your students to contact male celebrities, to ask what kind of books they like to read. Well-known comedians Ricky Gervais and David Walliams have written books that are very popular with boys.
- ✓ Get involved in the Reading Champions scheme, which is aimed at changing boys' attitudes to reading by using the power of male reading models. For more information visit www.readingchampions.org.uk.

Access to Reading for Children with SEND

Ensure that children who have special educational needs and disabilities have full access to books and reading. If you have a child in your class who has a hearing or visual impairment, talk to your special educational needs coordinator about strategies and ask for training to build your skills. Children who have a visual or hearing impairment will need opportunities to read books with large print, in Braille and in Sign Language. Children who have more severe impairments can use assistive technologies to communicate, such as the Eyegaze system described below.

✓ The RNIB offers books with large print and in Braille for children who have a visual impairment: www.rnib.org.uk/livingwithsightloss/reading/Pages/reading.aspx.
✓ My BSL Books offer an online library of books in British Sign Language. See www.mybslbooks.com/ for more details.
✓ The Eyegaze system is an assistive technology for people with disabilities. This system tracks a child's eyes to help them communicate. The child can generate speech by looking at control keys or cells displayed on a screen.

'Objects of reference' are very helpful for children with profound learning difficulties. The idea is to start with an object that has a particular meaning associated with it. For instance, a fork could symbolise food. When these objects are used consistently, they help the child understand what is going to happen – to 'read' their world through the use of objects. The child might move on from the object, to a symbol, photograph or other visual representation. These objects can also help a child express his or her choices and preferences through reaching, pointing and so on.

Reading Everywhere

Children who read for pleasure will tend to read whenever a spare moment presents itself – they want to fill every moment of every day with reading of some kind. Talk with your children about all the different places where they like to read, and whether they have ever read anywhere unusual. Do they like to read in the bath, the car, the train, the bus, in bed, on the beach, or somewhere else? Talk about the kind of conditions in which they like to read. Perhaps some students prefer music in the background, while others like silence? Many children love to read in the dark, perhaps under the covers with a torch, but some prefer to read outdoors in the sunshine.

Set up a whole school competition and challenge your students to bring in photos of themselves, reading in an unusual place. You could give prizes (of books or book tokens) for the best or most unusual entries. You might set this as part of a summer holiday challenge, to encourage your children to keep reading when they are not in school. Encourage staff to boost the profile of reading for pleasure in all areas of the curriculum. Just as we now expect that all teachers see themselves as teachers of 'literacy', so reading for pleasure has a place in every subject.

Reading Everything

Encourage your children to read all different kinds of texts, depending on what they enjoy. Yes, it is important to encourage children to read 'proper literature', but we must take care not to send the message that only some kinds of reading are 'of value'. When people read all different kinds of books or texts, they learn a lot about using the appropriate form and style for an audience, and about what does and does not work in writing. Make sure that you have plenty of different text types available in your setting and your library. Do an audit to make sure that you have as many different kinds of text available for your children as possible.

Check that your children have access to:

✓ comics, magazines and newspapers
✓ joke, quiz and puzzle books
✓ recipe books
✓ programmes from events (sports, theatre, etc.)
✓ poems
✓ short stories and graphic novels
✓ computer game guides
✓ character ('top trumps' style) cards
✓ dictionaries and encyclopaedias
✓ instruction manuals
✓ catalogues, pamphlets and brochures
✓ posters
✓ diaries and letters
✓ biographies and autobiographies
✓ ebook readers and reading APPs on tablets
✓ websites and blogs
✓ travel guides and maps

Interestingly, many students would not view reading these kinds of texts as doing 'proper reading', perhaps because they are less frequently used in schools. Question your own attitude to the value of reading these kinds of texts, to help you change the attitude of your children. And whatever it takes, keep trying as many strategies as you can, to ensure that all your children find a deep and lasting pleasure in reading.